How to Find Happiness In Yourself

25 Habits Guaranteed to Help You Live a Happier Life

Michelle Mann

from various sources. Please consult a licensed professional before attempting any techniques outlined in this book.

By reading this document, the reader agrees that under no circumstances is the author responsible for any losses, direct or indirect, that are incurred as a result of the use of the information contained within this document, including, but not limited to, errors, omissions, or inaccuracies.

Table of Contents

Introduction

Here you are, faced with the key to living a life of bliss and contentment.

All you need to really do is look within yourself and find the courage and strength to believe in who you are.

Precious time is passing along with the world around us, so why not join in on that ride by admitting your

Peace and acceptance to the present moment? Be patient and kind to yourself throughout this journey because inside you is the potential to do wondrous deeds!

In every person is the willpower, the focus, and the creativity to keep learning, striving, and growing into the best person they can be. Release yourself from the tensions of the past because

Newer and better things await you at every corner. Open yourself up to see the possibilities and graces that every day has to bring, and discover the different sides to every situation. Know that your mistakes and your shortcomings are not what defines you and that you always have the final say about who you are and how you choose to feel.

Every single person in this world has the right to be joyful about their existence. Know yourself and trust in the decisions you make because you are naturally a part of life.

Security of mind, body, and spirit are within your grasp. It is time to take charge of your individuality and live your life to the fullest.

Savor each and every moment of it!

Happiness

What is it about happiness that makes you long for its sensation?

Is it the satisfaction you feel that is accompanied by achieving a goal, or could it be the freedom you gain by releasing tensions from within yourself?

We all want it in our lives, but can we really see it coming?

Happiness, with its many meanings and forms, has been one of life's most precious treasures and may undoubtedly be the most sought out reward to every endeavor. Over the ages, people have searched for opportunities that could grant them the bliss of being in this state of mind. Yet, no matter how much they all try to fathom every detail of their undertakings, there just seems to be no fixed formula that can guarantee each one of us everlasting pleasure. We all work hard, we focus, we reach out to whatever might grant us the promise of happiness, but the funny thing is that when we think we have it within our grasp, we lose it. It is not just enough to say that we want to live a happy life, but we should resonate with this intention in all that we do and say.

Everybody has the potential to be happy on the inside, but that all depends on how much you want it.

We all experience happiness as more than just a handful of positive abstract feelings towards certain situations or people. We can feel it in our hearts, think about pleasant memories, and manifest positivity through our actions. Not only does yearning for happiness ring in our thoughts, but our own bodies actually want us to experience things that make us feel warm and giddy inside as well.

Our brains are powerful instruments that allow us to feel positivity. The happiness sensations are mainly caused by dopamine, endorphins, serotonin, and oxytocin—brain chemicals that produce feel good vibes that block negative things like agitation, pain, and sadness. A surge of happy hormones can make wondrous improvements to our productivity, like boosting our self-esteem in order to reach our goals, developing our talents with the prospect of self-improvement, and creating meaningful social bonds. But as delightful as this may sound, they can be dangerous if they are unbalanced and acquired through unnatural methods.

Our world today has produced commodified attractions that offer instant satisfaction, capable of fooling our brains into thinking that we are actually happy. Social pressures also muster the false importance of status, which defines a person's self-worth. It is toxic for us to keep up with this kind of unhealthy competitiveness because it only hinders us from being our true selves. Being happy is not found in the act of jumping from one merry moment to another, nor can we forcefully bring ourselves to feel immediate joy or delight when we think we need to. Give yourself some credit rather than tricking yourself into experiencing moments of happiness when you give in to urges or when you repeat habits that are harmful to your body and mind. Living a happy life is a process that requires you to be your authentic self every single day. Genuine happiness is lasting, fulfilling, and calls for you to look within yourself for that drive. Accepting your strengths and weaknesses and knowing your true value may be the surest way to determine what is best for you.

The prospect of happiness being a personal choice can be both relieving and daunting for two reasons: one— we control our emotions and feelings, and two—we may not be in control of ourselves and sometimes choose to give in to anxieties and stress. How certain you are of your entire self determines how you can cope with tough situations under pressure, which is really easier said than done. We have all been faced with challenges that make us question our capabilities and may be guilty of compromising ourselves in difficult situations. Sometimes we cannot help but change ourselves a little, and hopefully, it ends up being for the best. With all the surprises and uncertainty that the future holds, it always feels nice to be grounded by something constant—your ability to be patient and kind to yourself.

Beginning your own pursuit of happiness is much like training for the Olympics or running a race. With a goal that you may look towards as the beacon of your salvation. As far as one can tell, the many hardships and surface tensions in life are fleeting, just as the physical world continues to be in a constant state of transformation and change. You may realize that happiness, joy, satisfaction—all these positive and desirable feelings—may leave you when emotions at much greater levels push them away. A goal, once attained, passes as well.

Happiness is ultimately a state of mind that is characterized by peaceful thoughts, which means that it allows you to transcend the notion of physical time and space. Having a happy mindset can give you that extra push of hope when times get rough and help direct your attention to solutions that actually work. A person who is happy at the moment tends to be regardless of wanting and needing, and therefore feel like they have more than what they asked for. You may also notice that being happy can be 'infectious' and uplift the people around you.

Happiness can mean different things to different people depending on what they associate the sensation with, but it all boils down to feeling secure and at peace with yourself. It might not be too hard to admit that at times we long for that same vision and wish that we could carry it around to face the uncertainty of life ahead.

Discovering what it means to be truly happy feels like an awakening and may start out as the faintest whisper at the back of your mind telling you that "life means more than what is going on right now." Some people may experience this in moments of extreme stress when they feel that there is nothing else to hold on to but faith, while others might discover this awareness after going through the same problem a few times. This shift in your consciousness can bring you to see clearly if you allow yourself to accept things as they are. Hopefully, these twenty-five habits to find internal happiness can bring you to think of yourself and the things going on around you as, not by extremes but by a blend of everything else in between.

We are never going to get anywhere if we do not try.

We are slowly working to change our negative habits into positive ones each day.

We can make good and meaningful memories with our true friends and family.

We all embody happiness.

The Good Life

You picked up this book because you believe that you have the chance to live a good life and that you are hopeful of becoming a better person.

Life is experienced through the twists and turns of events that fill up the spaces between our beginning and end. It is initially presented to us without any promise of what is to come, except that things change. Life is a cycle of give and take, which does not necessarily mean losing and winning or success and failure. The game of life is an illusion that compels people to measure self-worth by striving to be the best one in the room. Still, there is no such thing as winning against others because of how different each person is.

Anything can happen.

Thinking about living the best life that you can means you have to be open to change outside and within yourself, which entails gaining and letting go of certain things. Think bigger and deeper than what you can acquire materially to see the more detailed connections between certain matters. The concept of gain and loss can be interpreted in numerous ways, such as shedding away self-destructive habits and negative personal qualities to make more room for self-improvement. You may be surprised to see how much people can change if you give them the opportunity to. Mischievous children might end up growing into respectful adults, while people who initially seemed to be unable to focus may turn into extraordinarily effective workers just by finding their niches. Take this time as an opportunity to explore your personality, talents, interests, and to develop your emotional skills.

Improving yourself does not entail you to lock yourself up in a cave or isolate yourself on the peak of a snowy mountain and meditate for the rest of your life. Life is about connecting, which means being around people, engaging in conversations, and forming genuine relationships. It also means finding yourself so that you can experience these moments authentically and to the fullest. You may be an individual but are ultimately part of something bigger. Have a sense of value and respect for yourself, as well as your ability to make an impact on others.

When we truly submit ourselves to life, we open ourselves to the bountiful gifts it has to offer and the possibilities beyond our limited perceptions. Unrealistic expectations that state that "every day will be a great day" will just make you disappointed. Just as constructing a self-image that suppresses your identity is an unfair standard to live by, stop seeing yourself as the victim to a bad situation or other people's criticisms, and start believing in yourself.

This very moment is the perfect opportunity for reinvention and experimentation.

Take it.

Chapter 1:

Thoughts About Happiness

The right time for you to be happy is always now.

Happy thoughts come from memories with positive experiences that allow us to identify what feels safe or pleasing to our senses. As opposed to this, negative experiences form into bad memories and make us dread similar incidents like them in the future. We naturally crave the good things in life but are also prone to being affected by harmful and discouraging events. Part of being human means that life may not always be luxurious and comfortable. We may be exposed to outside perils, that in turn, have the probability of characterizing our personal anxieties. Convincing yourself to overcome a toxic mindset does not have much of an impact if you force yourself to be happy but is rather acquired through a slow and formative process called *living*.

Thinking about happiness is just the beginning of a whole new perspective.

The paradox of living a happy life states that happiness can be found within you but also partly comes from how you perceive and interact with the world. Living life to its full potential would call for you to know yourself and nourish your talents in the best way possible to reach out to the world and make the changes you intend. Ideas and actions always work together to create progress, but if both of these factors cease to agree with one another, then it may stunt our growth as human beings.

Human behavior can be unpredictable at times, and this greatly affects how we make decisions. We can change our opinions in an instant if we encounter powerful words, or we could adopt new habits if we think that those tactics would help us survive better. Because of all the change happening around us, it can sometimes be difficult to pin down our emotions.

Have you ever experienced losing yourself and thinking you might never get out of a bad situation?

When an exaggerated notion of self-preservation reaches extreme limits, it turns a person into someone else entirely to avoid stress, panic, and paranoia. Although blocking out unwanted feelings serves as one way to deal with negativity. What it also does is pull you out of reality. Our thoughts are powerful forces that give us ideas on how to take things in new directions. If you choose to keep tricking your mind by giving in to momentary thrills or taking the easy way out. You may risk the danger of losing yourself and your relationships with others.

The present moment is the only time you have control over certain things, but mainly yourself. You are an instrument of hope, peace, and love. You have the potential to be creative and innovative when you embrace reality before you. Being happy allows us to feel comfortable with ourselves and gives us the assurance that tomorrow can be a new day to try again. Whatever situation you may be in, this exact moment can be something for you to learn from. Look around and allow yourself to be inspired by possibilities.

You are about to become the best version of yourself.

Smile

The way you put on a smile can dramatically change your outlook on a situation, not just because your facial expression might be slightly uncalled for, but for the fact that it introduces a different element to what is going on.

Have you ever thought about how laughter and jokes have the ability to momentarily break a train of bad thoughts and lift your spirits in a dull situation?

Humor has this remarkable quality of making people see reality for what it is. Not only does it give us something to crack up about, but pointing out something bluntly in a mild tone naturally eases the weight of a situation. Telling facts in a humorous way, like saying "listening to the silence is thrilling" instead of "don't ignore me," can break the ice and make that moment quite memorable.

Smiles and laughter give the impression that things may be less daunting than they actually are. A storm isn't going to destroy you if you know how to work your way around it. A bright comment takes us back to ourselves and gives our minds a break from overwhelming thoughts. Bringing life issues to the table with a bit of lightheartedness never hurt anyone. It rather allows us to confront tough situations by lifting their levels of seriousness. Have you noticed that happy-go-lucky people are generally more approachable than grumpy people? They seem more open to the world and are not as easily phased by danger or change. This does not necessarily mean that all problems are something to joke about or to be forgotten. Still, the power that a smile has to break the monotony of negativity can surprisingly shift the tides to any situation.

We all look out for the punchline of a joke or the unexpected turn of events at the end of a funny story. Because of this, we listen and pay attention to the elements around the narrative and even try to guess the outcome. For example, what do you brace yourself for when relatives come to attack? You may not know the end to this dad joke, but you may be willing to think ahead and analyze things in the storyline. In this case, relatives always mean family gatherings, and family gatherings mean getting together after a long time, so you might be bombarded with kisses on both sides of your cheeks.

Encountering the unexpected similarly leaves you almost defenseless to expectations before that event.

The difference between listening to a funny story and living in real life is that our emotions tend to be more complex in the latter experience, rather than just excitement or cheerfulness. Real life is also continuous, and each situation usually unfolds into other ones. Taking things one step at a time is a simple yet effective way to maximize your control over yourself and gives you the mental space to think about what you can do next.

Your ability to see a situation for what it is brings rise to your conscious awareness—the state of being aware of yourself as well as the things going around in your environment. Anticipating something makes you mindful about what is going on and always involves planning things along the way. Somewhat like multitasking, being consciously aware of everything allows you to see a situation from a bird's eye view while still maintaining your individual perspective. This naturally gives you the chance to move a situation forward by seeing more options to act on, as well as deciphering the best solution to tackle it.

Catching yourself unaware may sometimes give you insights into some things that you have not considered before. Your conscious awareness can be further strengthened by incidents like noticing someone else's reaction to that same event, or it may come to you in the form of a new idea. Keeping track of all these observations may give you the circumstances to mix and match the extent of your capabilities with whatever the situation calls for. Think of it as adding a new ingredient to a recipe that has the potential to drastically change its flavor and your impression of it. Doughnuts with either chocolate or vanilla filling might seem like a small difference, but some people really do prefer one over the other. A genuine smile is a physical feature that not only suggests optimism but is something that makes us feel restful inside.

Our minds and bodies are connected through purpose, which means we more or less do what we think. This happens as a unique process for everybody. Factors like personal background, personality traits, peers, and the relationship we have with our environment all contribute to our individual perspective. In most cases, we may find that these influential aspects of our life might hold conflicting views from one another. The challenge to bring the best parts of all of these things lies in your mind's ability to focus.

Acting courses have something called the "inner smile exercise," which are drills that help condition the artist's mind before performing heavier scenes. It works like meditation, which encourages you to focus specifically on happy thoughts. Embodying happiness can reflect as an outer glow on your face, even though you may not be smiling. Cases. Where we seem to be held back from wanting to do something means that our thoughts about prevention are much stronger than those about wanting to change. It takes time to heal yourself from feeling discouraged and hurt, but that does not mean that things will stay depressing forever. Just like the inner smile exercise, we all have the potential to train our minds to consider possibilities and manifest positivity into the things we do.

Being optimistic all the time should not be mistaken for blind positivity because that always leads you to making ungrounded decisions. Optimism entails being aware of your current situation and working with the limited available resources that you have to make the best out of it. Obtaining a positive mindset also does not necessarily call for you to put away unwanted thoughts for good, but rather to look at them more closely and see if you can spot any useful information that you missed. Organizing your thoughts might be a little bit overwhelming at first, especially if you feel strongly about certain matters. We all have experienced the inability to face people because of how angry we may have been at them or the struggle to impress someone on a first date because we wanted it to go perfectly. Our feelings and perspective make us human and allow us to experience life from a unique point of view. Letting your emotions clouds your thoughts and individuality and only makes you see one shade amidst an entire spectrum. It might take some time to get accustomed to seeing everything in full color, but being aware of the present moment is sure to bring out the best changes in you.

We can face the world with brighter eyes and work towards building a happier future.

Live A Life Of Virtue

To some of us, the concept of greatness might be far from reach. We might envision that as a goal, a personal quality to aspire to, or a state of living that appeals to us. We can sense the loop that society has held us in, which makes it more difficult to break free from routine. Some might view mundane tasks that fill our schedules as systematic and uninteresting, having no way of granting us the true meaning of life. There may be times when we look towards the horizon and wish that something or someone could just lift our burdens so that we may pursue the adventures we want to go on. Whether we realize it or not, we all believe in something greater than ourselves, and the only way to capture that is to first uncover who you really are.

To go beyond material wants and needs to find value in life is an idea that you first have to settle within yourself. You might want to feel happy and fulfilled, but working towards that goal may not feel quite right until you are in your most natural state. We cannot change the fact that our environment can cause changes to our disposition. People behave differently when they are under stress or anxious compared to when they feel safe. Being aware of yourself not only pertains to naming every feeling you have at the moment but also noticing how those feelings are affecting your views. Apart from knowing what you want and how to get there, it would be most gratifying to go through future challenges with your flair for things.

Think of a singer who makes a cover of a popular song and sings it as if they wrote it themselves. They might change the tempo, add a few adlibs, or tweak the lyrics a little bit to make it pass off as their own. Each singer has their own strengths—some may have high-pitched vocals, while others might have a unique texture to their voices. Others might opt for rapping, which is an entirely transformative take on music because it combines modes of conversation with the standard principles of singing. Each person confronts similar problems in different ways, and one of the major points to this is because we all have varying levels of personal traits.

We commonly perceive virtues as an abstract code of moral standard and are taught at a very young age to aspire to be virtuous. The reality is that virtues are not something you achieve, nor are they something that you have to fetch deep from within yourself. It is already what you are. We are all born with the same attributes, like the ability to love or control our temper, but the circumstances we go through from childhood to where we now determine how strongly we are able to enforce those characteristics. We generally know what is good from bad, but the experiences along the way have the potency to misplace certain meanings.

A common misconception of being good is that a person has to be soft-spoken, meek, and polite at all times—which really does not sound very realistic. If you see someone boisterously laughing in the hallway or disagreeing with whatever a teacher is saying, labeling those people as "not good" based on those perceptions is a shallow call. There is no such thing as a "purely good person" because everybody has depth and conflict within themselves. Artists know that tension in their work is what makes it more interesting. This concept does not always pertain to destruction or violence but may be something that challenges monotony. Things like using only one color to paint a picture or utilizing powerful brushstrokes are what makes an art piece stand out. Facing a terrible situation with a persevering attitude may, in turn, guarantee you a surprising outcome. How you respond to certain events, good or bad, might be the best way to decipher your character and hint you to your greatest strengths.

Living a life of virtue might call for you to face your fears because those are what hinder you from being your true self. Whether it may be a group of people you feel intimidated by or the culture of the job you are in. Take this as a time to find the strongest quality that you have in yourself and think about how being that kind of person affects your performance.

Once an artist releases their work into the world, they lose the right to tell people what to think of it.

There will always be more than one side to your story.

For example, being honest may help you clear things out with some people more easily but offend others even if you say things politely. A defensive reaction might be to keep explaining your point of view, or in a more extreme case, you might call that person out for thinking as such. You may also have the option to leave things as they are and go on with something else. Where would you put your energy?

Being human means that there is more to you than just skill sets and numbers.

Think of who you are when you are being your best self. This does not necessarily mean when you feel most powerful over others, but it is a trait that you gravitate towards naturally. A judge who carefully considers all aspects of a case might give an impression of being prudent, while a mother who talks to her misbehaving child instead of yelling may be considered as temperate. You might not always be managing yourself at your best, but there must be some pattern to your behavior that makes you want to reach out for the greatest good.

Uncovering your values is one step to becoming your true self and brings you a little closer to setting yourself free from the things that you are not. Negative situations are capable of making us act out of our natural character because of how much stress we are exposed to. We might think of playing tough because we do not want others to take advantage of us or prefer to keep quiet to stay out of trouble.

Society has created a space of interaction that standardizes our way of living. In most cases, entry-level workers may not always feel at their best when they are at their jobs. They might be afraid of messing up, and therefore feel restricted. They might be good at something, but their job does not necessarily need them to perform those skills. They might not be surrounded by people that they trust because of all the competition going on. Staying within that kind of space for a longer period of time would distance those entry-level workers from being themselves, especially if a company culture only advocates the value of sales. People who are able to deliver that cause flawlessly, but lack virtue, still risk destroying themselves at the expense of their genuine relationships with others.

Everyone has some sense of what other people are capable of doing.

If you go into a classroom and ask who the most hardworking student is, more or less everybody might point to the same person. Opposingly, if you ask everyone who they would not want to have in their group because that person does a terrible job at helping out, they might all point to that same person as well.

You can definitely learn about yourself from others, and sometimes talking to somebody you trust and who you are certain will have your back when things go wrong is the best person to bring out the best in you. Being true to yourself might not always give you the best treatment from the majority, but it is a quality that attracts people who have similar traits. People will react as they are accustomed to, which gives you insight into who they may really be. The foundation of a strong relationship lies in shared beliefs and values because those are what make people relate to one another. While balancing out a healthy friendship only works if there is mutual support.

We may give out as many favors as we can in friendships, but friendships are not made from favors.

If you are looking for a friend who is honest, supportive, loving, adventurous, humorous, and loyal—be that person first.

Find Something Worth Fighting For

We may all share the curiosity about the true meaning of life, and the secret is that you can decide for yourself.

Aligning your past, present, and future equals your purpose.

It is something deeply personal to each individual, and the reasons for it are rooted in our past. Have you ever had a collection of amazing memories that you longingly turn back to for a quick smile? What is a common positive feeling you had the moment you experienced those memories? Opposed to that, what memories bother you the most? Are they about your career, your family, or a personal relationship? How do you prevent them from happening again?

If you are able to piece together your perceptions about those matters, then you may have found what has majorly impacted your current outlook on life.

The present moment can be many things, but we are only entitled to one experience of it. Our individuality is an incredibly intimate experience of life, but at the same time is something that we can use to make a difference to the entirety of humanity. We have the ability to connect with our world and make use of its resources to create different kinds of lifestyles. Patterns of habit can be traced from every day you lived until now that can be used to predict where you may be heading for. Finding your purpose means more than "following your passion" or "doing what you love" because those factors can change. A purpose is constant and is the reason why you choose to continue living.

Having a purpose significantly shapes your future and is considerably classified under long-term endeavor. It is more than a goal and higher than an ambition. While the latter two fall under shorter-termed plans because they both have concrete ends, a purpose gives your life direction and does not necessarily connote a final destination. An ambition might be to become a pilot or a doctor, while goals that serve those ambitions would usually amount to graduating and earning a license. A purpose is not clearly defined by an event or an achievement but rather can be felt or found in the decisions you make. It is a conscious attitude that you bring with you that influences whatever you do in every situation that you encounter. Having a purpose in life can amplify so much meaning to the little things that we do each day because each step we take feels like we are getting closer to our final destination. Without a purpose, a person might feel like something is missing in their life. It may not be enough to just be a good person or to mindlessly keep achieving things. Being human means that we are all highly demonstrative creatures, and a purpose may be considered the top form of that expression.

Purpose is usually connected to concepts like intention, motive, cause, and aspiration, which all fall under long-term attainments. The irony of a purpose being intangible yet is something that binds our life together. It has the leverage to guide us to do what is right and help us see reason when something goes wrong. Since it entails foresight about how you would use your life to create the world you want to live in, living a life of purpose would call for you to balance out your motives both generally and objectively. This means having a vision, which is a clear enough dream to move towards. The main difference between a purpose and a vision is that a purpose answers your reasons for your pursuit, while a vision answers where you are heading.

You may notice how patterns of life can be associated with going on a journey and that having a vision can be like knowing your destination on a trip. For example, you may be riding a boat from island A to island B. Island B is where you physically envision yourself after some time of traveling, but your purpose may be to visit a family member. The waters you tread in between serve as the path, while your progress upon reaching island B is measured by nautical miles. Challenges, such as rough tides or lacking fuel, may occur during your trip and might cause a delay to your arrival. Still, your persistence on crossing over to island B lies with the thought of being reunited with family. Having a purpose prevents us from dwelling too much on negative things about the past, as well as holding on to misconceptions about certain events. We are able to pass over obstacles along the way because we see something that we want beyond it. Since we bring ourselves to focus on what we are aiming for, there is less room for being stagnant and more drive for progress.

During the early years in school, we may all have been asked to speak in front of a class, tell everyone what our vision for the world was and how we were going to achieve that. It sounds fairly simple, but many of us might have had unclear answers. The truth is that a purpose and vision might turn out to be quite broad because they entail the creation of a world that has not happened yet. To get to that final destination would mean trying out new connections to things or changing the rules entirely. A personal purpose and vision always have the capacity to extend on to others, so chances are that the people around you might share your dreams as well.

Sharing one purpose and vision can work for multiple groups of people. Whether it is to see everyone receive a good education or to advocate for world peace, people are able to relate to one another. Each person is entitled to their own beliefs, which sometimes makes them willing to join in on a strong common cause. Aligning your past, present, and future to reach your purpose is also an alignment of your values and personhood.

Try not to burden yourself too much about your life's purpose because that just defeats the reason for getting one. You were not meant to save the world on your own, and no one ever was. Begin with discovering who you are so that you can set practical boundaries for yourself and progress steadily thereafter. When you find that you are able to cope with obstacles along the way, you may notice that your advancement can boost your self-esteem. The confidence that you gain when you develop your abilities may help you use your strengths to balance out your weaknesses. You may find it easier to prioritize tasks on your schedule and things that make you feel like a better person. Letting go of pointless distractions that do not contribute to your well-being is a tremendous step you can take to make room for learning new things and expanding your views.

You are constantly going to be tested throughout your life, but when you strongly believe in something, you begin to work with passion. Passion does not seek for reward but is being in a constant state to serve and create. People who are passionate about their jobs are able to perform better and have greater chances of forming relationships with others. Living a life where we love what we do may sound like the best place to be, but it may not be entirely far from reach if we bring the people we love and care for along the way.

Other things to take into account might be to ask yourself if your chosen purpose can withstand the test of time. Do you think that the purpose you thought of is still able to be as clear and applicable when social, cultural, and economic changes occur? Or do you think it will be outdated in a decade or so? Are you able to resonate with others on this matter? If so, then how does the cooperation of others help advance your cause? What specific roles do you think people will have to take to help create your vision? If your purpose and vision do not involve the collaboration of others, then what other ways can your purpose and vision be of value to them? Lastly, will your purpose benefit the standards of living now or in the future?

Writing down your purpose, along with some goals that you wish to achieve, can be one of the most effective things you can do to make them come true. People are naturally visual beings, so seeing what you are after can be a great reminder for you to keep going on.

The physical world may change and pass, but what we feel inside and believe in can be lasting. As mentioned, a good and strong vision has the ability to outlive you and can be passed on to others to continue. Just how a country's foundation is built on values like equality, diversity, and love for its people does the message still rings over future generations. Ideally, leaders and citizens all try to move towards this vision, but the reality is that not every single person might have the privilege of experiencing those promises. It is possible that throughout time, attaining all of those dreams still may not become a total reality, but people in the times that follow still have the potential to resonate with those same principles.

Life may appear huge, surprising, and breathtaking, but what we experience each day always leads to something more.

Give yourself something to believe in.

Imagine All The Good Things

Imagining yourself as the best person ever proves that memory can turn into a highly creative endeavor.

The human mind is malleable and expandable, which means that our thoughts are never set in stone. They are composed of ideas, memories, desires, fears, rationality, and imagination. They all work together to process sensations and events that we encounter in our world. We experience real life in moments that are quick to transition to the next, which is why our memories continue to strangle with pinning down what actually happened. Surprisingly enough, our brains have a difficult time distinguishing reality from our imagination, and that explains why sometimes we still continue to think about things that have happened long ago.

Have you ever caught yourself reminiscing about the best summer you had in your childhood or recalling the fight that you had with one of your closest friends? You may notice that those memories still have the capacity to bring back some feelings from when you went through those events, and if they are vivid enough, you might feel that you were still present in that moment.

We are all attuned to telling what events belong in the past, present, and future, but since thoughts are not tangible things, they can overlap through time and space. Our minds allow us to bring back certain details to the present, where we sometimes live through them in order to understand them better. Regardless of whether a bad memory or a good one resurfaces in our thoughts, we all have feelings that we associate with those incidents, and those are what we continue to use to welcome or avoid similar experiences. Although we do not always remember the exact details of things that we experienced far into our past, like in childhood, we face them with our current knowledge with the intention of settling our minds about certain things.

Strong and vivid memories have the power to pull you deep into thought and re-experience the same or even amplified emotional responses that you had then. The danger of this may result in memory alteration, which is a defense mechanism used by the brain to help cope with stress and anxiety. The goal of this kind of endeavor is usually to hold on to the familiar from the fear of losing something or someone important to us.

Good things make us happy while bad things do not, but ironically we spend more time thinking about the bad things even if it might mean hurting ourselves. People register negative thoughts much longer than they do with positive ones. It is not because we are attracted to negativity, but because they induce a more complex set of emotions. Feelings of happiness and joy only encompass one side of the emotional spectrum, while those of disgust, anger, and guilt can compound and unfold into others. Probing our thoughts to alter that memory, or to generate other possible solutions to it, only leaves you with open-ended conclusions. You have no way of changing the past. Overthinking can drain your energy levels and hinder you from completing tasks. If you believe that details in a heavy or discouraging past experience can be of no help to what you may be going through now, it might be time for you to realign yourself with your purpose and vision for the future.

Your thoughts have the ability to attract opportunities to come your way. Setting your mind towards seeing the bright side of situations naturally opens you up to finding a solution or encountering somebody helpful. Unlike daydreaming, which entails us spending each day fantasizing about what will come tomorrow, take the challenge of turning your good thoughts into reality. A positive mindset does not always have to be about sunshine and daisies but is one that is willing to see reason, accept criticism as means for improvement, and be resourceful with whatever is available.

Our minds are capable of separating events from one another to understand things in a more collective manner. Shutting down certain aspects of our perceptions can be one of the most practical ways to concentrate. We may not notice it, but it is something that we do every day. Things like turning off your phone when you are at a meeting or shutting the door to our room when we go to sleep are some simple ways that indicate distancing ourselves from distractions. We have to accept that we may not all be able to juggle too many thoughts at once and that we might spend more time thinking about certain things than others. Although prioritizing your good thoughts may not always be easy, it is advisable to keep practicing and being aware of your current state.

Take the extra step to ensure your positivity by refraining from listening to those sad songs on your playlist or binging on heartbreaking romances on your television. Stay away from people who intentionally make you feel less than who you are, and learn to respect yourself more. Keep your back straight and chin up because you can do this!

You need to be aware of what filter you are using to approach situations. Talking to children and teaching them is most effective when we make use of speech in a positive voice. Saying things like "do not drink" or "cannot play" are only later registered by the mind after the child first captures the subject of a statement, which in those cases were the words "drink" and "play." Most likely, inattentive children would result in disobeying those rules because they only paid attention to the action words.

This tactic also works remarkably on adults. Were you ever so nervous about making a mistake on your first driving lesson? How did your mind respond to your coach when they said, "do not hit the obstacles?" Did it just make you think about the obstacles even more?

We may not be in total control of the outside world, but what we can do is train ourselves to keep our eyes on the road.

Imagining the good things does not only mean that we can look back to the past for consolation, but we can also reach out to the future for hope. The more you develop your ability to filter out bad thoughts, you may develop the ability to predict sounder outcomes. Ideas may not always manifest as you imagine, but the clearer your vision is, the more specific your efforts will go into attaining that goal.

There is so much more in store for you, and you can definitely turn happiness into a reality.

Motivate Yourself

Long-lasting happiness means your ability to be optimistic at all times—not to greet everybody you see with a smile, but to know that there is always something better that awaits you if you work consistently towards your goals.

Everybody needs encouragement.

It gives us a sense of security and the assurance we need to know if we are on the right track. Being appreciated by our parents and close friends, as well as having their beliefs can empower us to take risks, partly because we know we have support. As much we need to receive love from others, we must also learn to be faithful in our capabilities. Just like a purpose, your reason to be motivated is deeply personal and is based on what aspects you want to grow in.

Your enthusiasm for certain things can contribute to extremely powerful focus but may also waver depending on your mood. Being human does not entail waking up enthusiastically every morning to good vibes and big smiles because we all have bad days when we feel like we want to shut ourselves from the world. For whatever those reasons may be, our performance levels may not always be at our best.

Our moods change when we are put in different circumstances. Moreso, the longer we stay in those moods, the greater the chances there is of them becoming part of our personality. Your mood depends more on just your feelings about the weather, and learning about your responses might help you realize what makes you hesitant to confront certain things. Since being around other people is a huge part of our lives, try considering whether or not you belong within the culture that you are in. It may pertain to more than just not being comfortable around your peers; but might instead be the way you resonate with the vision and mission of the company that you are working for. Finding where you fit in in terms of purpose and vision can be highly impactful to your performance, but is understandably something that takes time to seek out and get to. Hopefully, this suggestion can be something you can work towards in the future and hopefully make yourself more certain of who you are.

Progressing in life always entails gently pushing your boundaries. Whether it may be learning a new language or approaching a coworker with whom you have difficulty connecting with, each step you take to make those positive changes entails self-growth. Facing challenges with a can-do attitude can also spread to others around you and can attract like-minded people to join in on your adventure. Getting something done perfectly does not always happen instantly, but nonetheless, there are always small nuggets of life lessons to earn from every situation. Be reasonable, and give yourself enough time to accomplish the tasks that you need to do. Half-baked skills produce half-baked outputs, so it may be best to learn new things until you are confident enough to share them with others.

In some cases, we may not care whether or not we do a good job at something. Feeling discouraged from criticism and not trying means that we lack interest and that our hearts are just not in it. Sustaining your motivation to reach your goals sometimes means doing things that you are not enthusiastic about. You do not eat a pie by taking out all its filling and leaving the crust, or vice versa—it is all or nothing.

People procrastinate for different reasons, but it all boils down to knowing what you care about the most. What all creative jobs have in common is reigniting that spark of inspiration and trying to carry that energy throughout all their projects. If you feel that your talents and abilities were meant for something else specifically, find time to do those things on a regular basis if you are not ready to turn it into a career just yet. You are not failing; rather you may not be motivated.

The key is to keep the momentum going, no matter what.

Know what distracts you, and set new goals for yourself. Write your plans in a journal, or create a to-do list to remind you of your daily tasks. This reduces some strain in your mind from overthinking, so that you can use that energy for more important things.

Reciting positive affirmations daily can be a fun way for you to get creative with your words, apart from giving you that extra kick of self-esteem. Saying encouraging things out loud that are directed to areas where you think you need a confidence boost helps you look at yourself much more lightly and shifts your mind to see your strengths.

Your physical health matters just as much as your mental state, so give yourself a break when you need to. Small things like fixing your posture not only improves the blood flow to your brain but are ways to show the world that you are proud of who you are. Maintaining good physical hygiene, such as brushing your teeth at least twice a day and taking regular warm showers or baths, can loosen our muscles and help us relax after a hectic day at work.

The well-acclaimed practice of daily meditation helps you lengthen your attention span by focusing on only one thing: breathing. Not only would you be training your lungs to expand more, but you may be surprised at how easier it may be to prioritize your options and make sounder decisions. Try it for a week, and note of any changes or improvements that you notice about yourself.

Do this for yourself, and feel good about it!

Trust Yourself

Whatever choice you make sets you on a definite path, and you would never know how the other options would have played out.

Making decisions is something that we do every day. Whether it is life-changing, like selecting what course to take for college or something simple, like deciding what to have for breakfast. Our entire life is shaped by the choices we make. We are only entitled to drawing one path for ourselves, and that means that everything we do may be accounted for. We naturally gravitate towards choosing an option that benefits us the most, but when the choices we make seem unclear about how they define our future, our inability to take control gives rise to self-doubt.

Overthinking the "what ifs" to other choices you could have taken only magnifies what you give your attention to. This has the tendency to bounce off onto other thoughts that feel real but might never even come true. Overthinking is exhausting and lessens your brainpower to think about other things. If you are planning on making big changes to your life, thinking too much about every single outcome might eventually convince you to not make that decision.

The truth is that you may never have a guaranteed outcome to anything and, no matter how clear you think you foresee the near future, unexpected things can still happen. We all can aim to give ourselves some peace of mind by learning to give allowance to the outcomes we predict. Since we all know that nothing is certain, we can bring ourselves to find something to be grateful about rather than wallowing in disappointment if things do not go as expected.

Decisions that could significantly change the course of your life are the ones we spend the most time thinking about. Talking about your feelings to a close family member or friend whose opinions you value may be the most practical way to pick the best option. Even though you may seek outside help, you would need to know yourself before you take any advice. Balancing out other people's opinions with your self-views can be a great way to find the equilibrium to your capabilities. Ask yourself how taking on this endeavor would help you grow into a better person. Do you find the idea of it delightful and thrilling? What was the basis of your choice? Do you think it will boost your status, or are you doing it to please others? Furthermore, would the choices you make hurt anyone and do you have the time, skills, and funds to make it happen?

Being certain of yourself, you can raise your ability to take more control over a situation. We are all trying to build healthy self-esteem, and the only way to do that is to start making some good choices for ourselves. Surely you have developed talents and skills that you can be proud of. Allow yourself enough time to think about things for now, and learn to put them off when the situation calls for it. You do not have to make the perfect choices to live the best life; but instead, you can trust in your abilities as well as call on others when the time calls for it.

Self-confidence comes from your experiences. A child develops healthy self-esteem when their parents, teachers, and friends are supportive of them. It does not mean that they were only praised and congratulated all their life, but were taught to weigh things out for themselves. We build self-confidence by constant exposure to the world around us—facing people, taking on challenges, finding newer and better ways to do things. This is not to be mistaken for conceitedness. Being confident means that you are certain of doing something well enough and are proud of your talents. Contrastingly, being conceited means that you think you can do something better than the other person. Apart from putting others down, harboring this attitude always results in unhealthy competition. Being confident in yourself reflects outwards into the things you do. Chances are that others will see that and may put their trust in you as well. Being confident in yourself allows you to share the things you have learned and not worry about losing them or becoming less of a person because of it. Having good self-esteem naturally allows us to reach out to others and take certain measures to help others trust in themselves.

We all want answers, but the reality is that there is always more than one.

Scrolling down the list of movie choices and watching every single preview until your total time doing that amounts to a full length film can amount to either two things: you can be a little indecisive, or you just love watching previews.

Practicing decisiveness with small matters first can help you gain confidence for taking larger steps later in life. Learning how to make decisions under time constraints while considering other factors around can eventually lead you to take bigger risks. You can start right now, like picking what you want for dinner or choosing your outfit for the next day. For now, it does not matter what other people think.

Just pick something!

Love Yourself

Accepting yourself for who you are might sometimes be the hardest thing to do.

We all have thorough access to the extent of our flaws, our emotional weaknesses, and our deepest and darkest secrets that we sometimes feel ashamed of leaking out into the world. We all have times when we feel discouraged and tend to put the blame on ourselves for not being good enough. Living every day with the knowledge of uncertainty and limitations can be frightening if we continue to hold on to that idea. Just as bottling up those feelings of anxiety and hurt without trying to deal with them might as well result in their growth and permanence. Learning to love yourself, just like anything in life, is a process that takes time and effort, but it is all worth it once you begin to see the world in a brighter light. Just as we are encouraged to share the beautiful things about ourselves, we might have to let go of our negative aspects in order to transform them into better qualities.

The world today can be quite hectic and demand so much of our energy. Because of this, we may be tasked to do things that may not be in our expertise or to our liking. Being exposed to criticism from others can greatly affect what we think we are capable of. If we are still on the journey of learning about ourselves, then we might experience confusion as to what actually matters to us. The truth is that you may not think that you deserve love and acceptance outside if you cannot bring yourself to love and accept who you are on the inside.

Loving yourself is not to be mistaken for selfishness or conceitedness, which calls you to be dependent on outside factors to feel good. Allowing yourself to be carried away by trends or judged by other people does not amount to the individuality you possess. Those elements to life are fleeting and trifle compared to the value of your skills and personality. You may be inclined to certain things, but none of those can ever come close to defining the creativity and vibrancy within you. You can choose what to do with this outside information and construct them in a way that you think represents you best.

Know where you stand because only then can you be in touch with your full potential.

Take some time to be with yourself each day to check how you feel about being yourself. Since time always brings about new opportunities, you might find your list of characteristics growing. Some traits may be desirable, while you might want to rid yourself of others, but you always have it in your power to balance out those qualities when a situation calls for it. We may not be completely satisfied with ourselves at certain times, but that just means that there is always room for improvement.

Be kind and patient to yourself, even when you do not think you are worthy of it. You do not have to live up to the unrealistic expectations you put up for yourself, as well as those that others put on you. Developing healthy self-esteem takes more than posting a few of your best camera-ready pictures on social media or buying yourself new things on a regular basis. We all know that outward love may not always be available, nor is it always long-lasting. In instances where we might need to face things alone, taking charge of those situations would always call for us to trust in our senses and occasionally our gut feelings.

You might need to revisit your past to a certain extent to be able to understand the patterns of your decision-making skills. A person begins to develop self-esteem as early as in their childhood, through the people who surrounded them and the environment they lived in. We all need to make the journey to go beyond surface-level reasoning and to turn to ourselves for peace. Sometimes having a problem pertains to the situation around you and not who you are. Taking things too personally is bound to inflict you with unnecessary pain that may eventually develop into chronic self-doubt. If you think about everything too seriously, you might risk feeling humiliated even if you did nothing wrong. We always hear things like "the only way you can help others is if you put yourself first" or "the only way you can give true love is when you learn to love yourself fully," which if you come to think about it, actually makes sense. You cannot give encouragement to others if you do not believe that challenges can be overcome, nor can you take care of others if you are physically weak or sick.

We can either view limitations as something that stops us from reaching our goals or as a boundary that we have to maintain until we have enough strength to cross it. Grade levels in school were made for this precise reason. It would be impractical to accelerate to a level six from a level four if we had not mastered our subjects yet, while nothing could guarantee the replacement of experiences we would miss at a level five. Taking on too many tasks at once can burn you out and cause you to produce bad quality outputs or not finish tasks. Saying "no" can be much better than giving out empty promises to others and can be a better way to keep good relationships. Take enough time to develop the skills that you need to on your own. This will benefit you in the long run. Take the opportunity to improve on your speaking skills and explain your situation kindly to them. You may be surprised to know that other people can be patient and understanding when it comes to these things.

Loving yourself may help you feel more comfortable when you come to face challenges or are stuck in bad situations. Instead of running away from what you think you are unable to handle, being confident can open you up to learning new things.

Try setting an intention for yourself each day. It does not have to be too complicated or grand. Pick an attitude that you think would be useful to tackle the things you need to do, or something that can contribute to your emotional or social growth in general. Be as specific as you can, and keep it to one intention per day as to not overburden your thoughts. Maneuvering throughout your schedule with more self-awareness could bring you closer to the present moment, where you may discover that there is so much to be grateful for.

Chapter 2:

Happiness On The Go

It is not about the magnitude of a single event that has the capacity to change your life, but the little things you repeat every day that manage to shift the direction of where you are heading.

Constancy forms habits, which are one of the main characteristics of people. We all act and speak through certain patterns, are inclined towards particular styles, and are attracted to people who we think would match our own personalities. Each individual has their own unique set of traits and behaviors that somewhat gauge how they interact with their environments, and this continues to develop with each passing day.

Attaining an optimistic mindset takes more than just thinking about being happy; but requires you to take action to complete the happy experience. You get into shape by exercising for twenty to thirty minutes every day and by sticking to a diet with lots of nutritious foods. You do not study for twelve hours and finish a course, but take around three to four years of learning and research until you finally deserve to receive your college diploma. It is impossible to truly love a person in just one day because it takes time to get to know every bit about them. Being happy is a process that involves getting to know yourself fully, and discovering things that you didn't know before.

The culmination of all your little efforts to be the best version of yourself shapes more than just your outlook on life, but may influence your reality as well. Finding your own beat might be a little rough at first, but only because you may be testing out new things and are discovering how to approach situations in your own way.

Keep being yourself and take on opportunities that allow you to branch out to see differences and possibilities. One day, you may realize your perfect fit into the flow of everything else.

Express Yourself

Getting on a rollercoaster means being able to scream at the top of our lungs once we get to that highest peak, without anyone telling us to hush up. Whether it is a sense of freedom you are experiencing or a serious case of nausea, that scream is telling the world how you feel on the inside.

There is something remarkable about being in different places that reveal other sides to ourselves. Like how we can be extremely loud with our close friends at one moment, then shut ourselves off from the world with a hot cup of cocoa on a rainy night the next. It might be more than just a mood swing but can be interpreted as how our senses perceive the present moment. Those days when we feel extra friendly might not apply to all days, and our inclinations can waver depending on whether we are in the mood for rollercoasters or cocoa. There may be some things that we are easily comfortable doing and others that take quite a while to get used to. Nonetheless, all those small details still amount to who we are and how we interact with the world.

Personality and behavior are curiously adaptable concepts because we all bounce off these things from one another and yet are still able to maintain a sense of who we are. We all have elements of being introverted and extroverted, depending on where we are and who we are with. We are capable of personal growth and are not limited to being described by a handful of characteristics. Because of this, going beyond experiences in our comfort zones gives us the audacity to do remarkable and astounding things. Who would have known that the shyest person in the room might actually not be frightened to perform a musical number on stage?

Each person is like a different color palette and is their own unique blend of personalities, talents, culture, desires, and so much more. We all have different styles of walking, distinct voices, different levels of optimism—even twins have different fingerprints. All those traits were meant to be brought out into the world for us to understand and manage them as we wish. It is a quality of perception that calls for us to move around to know ourselves and promote interaction.

We all need the opportunity to be seen, heard, and understood.

As social beings, expression means that we also need others to perceive us. It is in our biological nature to require attention, to be assured by the company of others, to be congratulated when we achieve success, and to be amongst the people who we love and care for. Events such as birthday parties, graduation ceremonies, and family reunions all celebrate a person's passage from one stage in life to the next. With that comes joy and pride from everyone who is part of the gathering.

Serotonin is a hormone that is responsible for generating those feelings of fulfillment and status, and it also helps us reinforce relationships with one another. It is why we experience mother-daughter and as student-mentor bonds, friendships, and brothers in arms kinship. Serotonin gives us that sense of security when we are able to connect with other people. The amazing part is that not only do you feel it within yourself, but the sensation is mutual in others as well.

If you have all those great qualities within you, share them and allow others to improve themselves by your example. People can be gifts to one another while observing others and admiring their good traits encourages you to become a better person. The more you exercise your individuality, the more you may find other unique ways of expressing yourself. Holding back your talents and not being able to talk about your feelings causes you stress because it partly hinders you from being the person you are supposed to be. Being able to love yourself means that you need to be proud of who you are and feel a sense of belonging with those who matter to you. It is not about showing up to social gatherings enumerating your credentials one by one, or telling people how many friends you have.

Being yourself makes you stand out from a crowd. People always sense it but are not always able to explain why. Ironically, being natural makes you distinct because you would be able to interpret things in a special way. Art is something deeply personal and is produced from the relationship between your personhood, your craft, and your vision. It is a type of communication that does not always entail one-on-one contact with others but has the ability to impact society as a whole. Exhibits are held to showcase these pieces for others to find pleasure in, and to some extent, help them see another side to life. People gravitate towards honesty, no matter how distorted it may be. Just like films are premiered in theaters while music can be enjoyed in everyone's homes, These modes of expression grant us access to some person's view of the truth, and that in itself is extremely exciting.

You were born with natural gifts and have learned so many new things along the way. If you cease to express yourself to the world, then what you might have been capable of showing just ends up staying as an idea.

Your individuality means that much, and the world needs to hear it.

Let us open ourselves to be the best that we can be, and see the best in others.

We all have something to share.

Make Me-time A Regular Thing

Imagine a world where you brought your work home, ate meals, and chatted with your friends all at the same squashed-up time. Does it sound familiar? If you are guilty of this, like most of us might be, it may be time to reconsider shutting your phone down and spending some real time for yourself.

We all need some time to get to know ourselves better, and it feels just like running back into an old friend.

There may be instances when we all think that we are not completely ourselves. Whether it might be something bothering you or if you just feel emotionally and mentally drained, it happens to everyone, and that is just fine.

The good news is that it is not chronic and that we always have the ability to know what feels right and what does not.

Making me-time for yourself is all about strengthening and regaining your identity and going back to doing the things you love. It is as simple as setting a fine line between your work life, the time you spend with your family and friends, and for yourself. Me-time should be all about relaxing and de-stressing from the outside pressures, reaching out to your own uniqueness, and recharge for the days ahead.

What excites you? What is something that you have wanted to try out for but never had the courage to? This is the perfect time to look into yourself and reignite that creative spark.

Set some time for yourself after each day, or give yourself an entire day off out of the week to unwind. Try to stay awake if you can, and let your mind do minimal work on the things that please you. The value of disconnecting can be just as important as learning how to connect with the world while setting the right time for everything can prevent you from getting brain drained.

You can also think of me-time as maintaining personal privacy because truthfully there are just some things that you would like to keep to yourself. Sometimes, being in isolation gives you the freedom to do what you want without being conscious that other people may be watching. Apart from giving yourself something to look forward to, being with yourself can develop your ability to concentrate better. You may find that creating space for yourself can help you think more clearly, especially when you are planning on making bigger decisions.

Spending time with yourself can help you form better relationships with others while staying true to your character helps you find other people who can complement your personality. Best friends do not always agree with one another but still, choose to be together because their differences make that relationship exciting. By having a strong sense of identity and by being yourself, you can allow others to love you for who you are.

Get A Hobby

Since you have already made it this far into finding happiness within yourself, why not spice it up with a fun, recreational hobby?

Getting the right amount of busy each day can be a healthy start to maximizing your life experience. Apart from spending time at work and relaxing at home, a hobby allows you to branch out into other fields and adds depth to your skillset. Have you ever noticed how everyone seems to be in awe at people who play musical instruments or take on sports? Not all of them might be amazing at what they do, but we cannot deny that having a hobby is pretty darn admirable.

The concept of recreating yourself implies personal and social growth, which means that this could be a great way for you to form new relationships as well. They are a wonderful way to stay active and keep thinking, as well as maintaining a good emotional balance. A hobby can also help you gain self-confidence over time and can spark out new interests in you.

Be reasonable with how much time that you have on your hands, and pick something that you can easily slip into your daily or weekly schedule. You might also want to consider how much you are willing to let go from your budget, as well as whether or not you would like to continue this hobby when you transition into retirement.

Have you ever considered doing comedy? Being around a crowd of people who just want a good laugh can be the best way to get your spirits up. Apart from getting a full charge on positive vibes, you may get some new ideas on how to interpret the world.

There are so many hobbies out there just waiting for you to pick up.

Do something that strongly reflects who you think you are.

If you like moving around and are aiming to get physically fit, try considering sports, dancing. Yoga, in particular, is designed for you to gain strength at your own pace and improve your concentration. Outdoor activities like canoeing, rock climbing, hiking, and swimming can also be a great opportunity to enjoy nature and is a chance for you to connect with others as well. These physical hobbies can help you develop a healthy attitude towards competition, as well as can help foster values like teamwork, patience, endurance, and respect.

Board games, sudoku, and puzzles all help improve your strategic skills and train you to endure long hours of concentration. If you are looking to expound on knowledge, consider reading in a new genre or taking a class. Sharing and bouncing off your ideas with others can turn into something inventive, and open ourselves to other people's perspectives. On another note, book clubs and doing community work also give you the chance to fully engage with others and learn about their life stories. They also strengthen community bonds and make each one of us feel a sense of belonging.

Creative hobbies can range from crafts like sewing and crocheting to fine arts like painting, sketching, and sculpting, which all improve hand-eye coordination and observational skills. Playing a musical instrument not only stimulates almost all the parts of your brain but is a wonderful way to express yourself. Cooking and baking can be just as creative as poetry or creative writing because you can totally change up recipes and make them your own. And for those lovely people out there who are passionate about makeup and hairstyling, try taking your skills a step further by volunteering at your local theater to do some styling. You may be surprised how putting your skills in a new environment can amplify your ability to think outside the box.

The list does not stop here. Go out there and find something that truly captures your personality.

Do not be afraid to be bold. It's never too late to learn something new!

Eat Healthy

"You are what you eat," they say—and it might be partially true.

Biting into a double-double and having extra fries on the side might feel extremely satisfying, but having your three basic food groups in one meal just elevates your spirits to a whole new level. Not only would you have been proud to control your urges, but you would also be assured that you did your body well.

What you put into your body greatly affects your physical status, as well as your mood. We may all have been taught at an early age in school to take our meals regularly and stick to a balanced diet, and there are good and sound reasons for it. The three basic food groups—go, grow, and glow—are the best fail-safe eating tips we can take to ensure that we have enough energy to last us for the day. Getting the right balance of nutrients would also help repair cell growth and strengthen our immune system.

We all want to live happy lives, and the only way we can enjoy it is if we can actually get up and explore the world for ourselves.

Have you ever met anyone who rejoiced at the sight of their hospital bill?

That just proves how much we need our health to be happy.

Food is extremely important for us to survive, but it can also be something we enjoy. We all probably love to eat out with family and friends, because meals are just better with the people we love. Sticking with a regular meal schedule, like eating your breakfast, lunch, and dinner on time, as well as budgeting your portions. This may be the most practical way to maintain a good diet. Your body craves routine, so it might need to exert more effort to keep in balance if you skip meals regularly. This could result in long-term disorders and weight gain.

Staying away from foods and drinks that are rich in preservatives, sugars, and bad fats can be dangerous for your system. You may want to consider that as you age, your ability to physically heal might decline. Starting to care for yourself now might reduce your risks of getting critically ill.

Take this as an opportunity to try new things. Meal preparation can actually be quite exciting, and dining can be even more rewarding if you cooked the food yourself. The kitchen is not a scary place but it can be a space to get creative and polish up on new skills. Do not feel discouraged about your recipes if they do not look picture perfect just yet. Enjoy yourself, and improvement will come along in time. Suppose you already love cooking and baking and are quite good at it. In that case, you may like the idea of exploring other cuisines and may surprisingly find recipes that actually suit your taste.

Drinking enough glasses of water each day, and having some fresh juices every now and then, can contribute to good gut health and can hydrate us on a cellular level. They are the best natural cleansers, can reduce migraines, and protect your skin. It may be best to read a book that specializes in natural juicing if ever you decide to have a go at it. Drinking warm water also helps cool you on the inside, while inhaling its steam can soothe your nasal passages and cleanse your lungs.

Interestingly enough, color actually has something to do with how much nutrients are in food! Of course, this only pertains to natural foods and not those with artificial coloring, like in most desserts. The more colorful the palette on your plate is, the better chances you are at having all the nutrients you need. A colorful plate of food also looks inviting and makes you more enthusiastic about eating!

For those of you who do not really want to bother yourselves with counting calories or abiding by overly strict diets. You can try approaching your local nutritionist to create a meal plan that best suits your body type.

Be excited about making good changes for yourself because eating well does reflect on the outside.

Move Around

This is the part of the book where you see the heading and subconsciously get up to move, but then remember that you are still in the midst of reading this section and have to sit through it for a bit longer.

As human beings, we all have a yearning for adventure and excitement in our lives. It shows in the books we read and the movies we watch that our imaginations crave new sensations and sceneries. Sometimes, an escape through our minds can be a nice way to deal with cases of information overload, but nothing beats spending some time going out and doing it ourselves.

Moving around is a great way to quickly release any built-up tensions in your body. We were all made with bones and muscles, and it proves that we need some form of physical activity. Each working cell in your body produces energy, and letting that sit within you can make you feel restless and anxious when you might not have any reason to be. The body releases stress hormones called epinephrine and norepinephrine, which can instantly energize us and lift our moods. Apart from improving your blood flow, staying active gives you the opportunity to strengthen your immune system and grow more resilient. If you are new to this kind of lifestyle, don't be afraid or hesitate from adding movement to your daily routine because taking the time to stretch regularly and be active does guarantee you the benefit of living a longer and happier life.

The right amount of regular exercise that suits your build has been proven to bring lasting benefits to strong bone, muscle, and redeveloping certain brain structures. It also keeps your heart pumping, strengthens your lungs, and can ease your body into staying fit for old age. Sweating helps cleanse your skin by flushing away cellular debris while releasing pent-up emotions through movement can contribute to a better temperament. While some of us might not be as athletic as we hope to be, you do not have to perform high-intensity workouts to be considered a healthy person. Yoga is a great option that allows you to strengthen yourself at your own pace, and the best part is that you can do it at the comfort of your own home.

Exercising is not limited to workouts at the gym but can pertain to other forms of physical training. Team sports like basketball, soccer, and baseball all foster cooperation, trust, and can increase your confidence. In contrast, solo sports like running and swimming can help you improve your motor skills and mental toughness. Although allotting twenty minutes to an hour of exercise a day has its benefits, it does not compensate for long hours of sitting. It may be best to take little breaks from your work from time to time, like standing up and stretching every ten minutes or so. Small movements like lifting your heels, looking away from a monitor screen, or just changing your position in general still contribute to your overall wellness.

Remember to always listen to your body and not push yourself too hard when you feel tired. Physical activities are meant to make you healthier and happier. That does not happen by suffering from muscle pains the day after a workout. Endorphins are one of the happy hormones in your brain tasked to mask physical pain, which means that your body will always try to back you up when you are doing rigorous work. You may feel amazing while running on a field, and pushing your limits, but it may always be best to come home feeling renewed and energized at the end of the day.

Movement is how we connect and make changes to the world around us, and through that, we gain a deeper understanding of how our body and mind works. In some ways, we learn from activities like studying and reading that are meant to be applied outside. Apart from exercising and sports, connecting with nature and traveling are other pastimes that allow you plenty of time to walk around and indulge in different sights. Just be sure that the activity you choose is within your budget and can easily slip into your schedule.

Going from one place to another can be refreshing to our senses while being in new spaces can help generate fresher connections to things. Seeing the world from different angles, and not just through our phones, is where the real excitement is at, especially if we choose to bring along our closest friends and dearest family members.

We can achieve the things we set out for, and what it takes is to get up and go after it.

Declutter

Your living space is a reflection of who you are.

People are naturally visual beings, which entails absorbing the details from our surroundings. This partly affects how we feel and behave. The state of our environment can greatly make an impression on our moods and habits, and believe it or not, a cluttered space could potentially contribute to feeling unproductive and sullen.

We are all aiming to be happy and peaceful, and that means being well-rounded and improving ourselves in any way we can.

How can you get your job done if you cannot find something that you need, and how could you forget about sad memories if you still have loads of pictures that remind you of that event hanging from your walls?

Make your space a reflection of who you are.

You do not need to own a mansion to create an amazing personal space, and the place where you are living should do just fine. Pick a spot where you think you would like to retire to, to think, or be creative. It could be a room with a view, or somewhere you could get loads of sunshine—and it does not have to be limited to your bedroom. If you enjoy cooking, then your kitchen deserves all the love you can give. If you enjoy being outside, tending to a garden or styling your backyard can be a wonderful experience to connect with nature. People who do yoga at home usually design their own little gym at the corner of a room, and those who love painting might love staying out on the balcony all by themselves. Make a space where you could recharge yourself from work or from your social life. If you have a home job, it might be a good idea for you to personalize your workspace to give you that extra motivational kick.

Redecorating can be an excellent way to refresh your area, and is an activity that you do not need to splurge on. Rearranging your things, as well as getting rid of those that you do not need, can be an inventive way to maximize your living space.

Get your priorities straight! It's time to clear up your mind.

Suppose you intend to become a graphic artist or a musician. In that case, it seems that you are not going to need an MD in physical medicine to pursue careers in those fields, and would only require to specialize in skills specific to your profession. There are just some things we need to let go of in order to follow our own paths. Accumulating loads of information because you think it will be useful one day cannot serve its purpose if you cannot find a way to express that with an impact.

Why buy a shirt if it does not reflect your personal style?

Decluttering can save you the trouble of overthinking and brighten up your mood. Plus, clearing your space gives you more room where you could invite your friends and family over and talk about the good things.

Just give it a try!

Get Enough Rest

Resting your eyes will never be as good as resting in bed.

Job demands and running errands may take up most of our day, and the idea of repeating those tasks might sound dreadful without the idea of a break. We all spend so much time working and being about life that we end up sacrificing some of our basic needs. We live in a world where work and our personal lives continuously overlap, and sometimes it makes us feel that there is not enough time for everything.

Being happy results in creating a schedule that can take care of all your basic personal needs, while living a good life means trying to find the balance between everything and sometimes having to teeter within a zone of acceptable allowance. New things happen each day, and the best way to take advantage of those experiences is if you are ready to welcome them.

Overworking puts us at risk of getting burnouts that sometimes feel even worse and last longer than hangovers. Not only does it damage our long-term health, but it cuts down your momentum as well. For those people out there who say that they love their jobs, it is good to know that you are passionate about what you are doing, but a well-deserved break from it all can refresh your mind. It also gives you some distance to think of better ideas and newer strategies to further push your progress.

We all want to perform at our best, but we may cease to work efficiently if we feel drained and sick. Relying on caffeine, energy drinks, or medications to give an instant boost of energy to your body only has temporary effects. These are not advisable for long-term use, as they increase our heart rate, give rise to high blood pressure, and cause dehydration. The longer we overindulge ourselves with these rest replacements, the more prone we can be to experiencing insomnia. They increase our feelings of anxiety, stress, and damage our internal organs as well. For coffee enthusiasts, limiting yourself to one cup a day can be the best way to keep your body in balance.

Our body has the ability to naturally heal and rejuvenate itself, and getting enough sleep can be a lifesaver. Sleeping at the exact time every day helps your body get accustomed to a routine, which in the long run helps you think and act more efficiently. Our diets also affect our sleeping patterns, so minimizing your sugar and salt intake, especially during the hours when you intend to wind down, can help regulate your body's energy flow. If you enjoy warm drinks, having a cup of chamomile tea before bed can help relax the tension within you.

You might not need to haul yourself out of bed every morning with a good night's sleep. Try these tips out for a week, and see if you like the results. Always make time for yourself to feel your best, stay healthy, and make your bed!

Chapter 3:

The Bigger Picture

Our connection to the world around us is what defines our existence.

The air we breathe, the water we drink, and the sunshine we get all greatly benefit our well-being, but the people you choose to surround yourself with matter just as much.

Perfection does not exist because change happens every day. Not all days are good days, and parts of life can be filled with things that frustrate or harm us. All of those things are here to stay, but how you choose to face them creates the distinction to your personal story.

You are more than capable of channeling your happiness outwards and opening yourself up to let it flow through you.

The cycle of giving and receiving is what life is about, and that in itself indicates movement. Finding the balance amongst things does not mean hitting the bullseye or holding yourself steady in one position, but instead being able to wobble, weigh, maneuver, and sometimes even stagger within an acceptable zone of compromising. Being able to make confident decisions lies in the relationship you have with yourself and with the people who make up your support system.

We all strive for things like cause and belonging because it gives meaning to our existence. This is what it means to experience the path that lies between the starting line and finish line on a race track. Life is about action and excitement, and we search for these experiences to feel good about ourselves. Being a part of a group or a community that matches your values and beliefs can set you free from anxieties. While allowing others to open up and share their experiences with you, and vice versa. The exchange of experiences may potentially manifest into remarkable undertakings.

Being with people means that we have the opportunity to see life from a greater perspective, while factors like diversity and acceptance all fill in the gaps in our personal views about things. We may be brought together by our commonalities, but we stick together because of our differences. Inclusion means more than just accessibility, which only connotes letting people in but is a system that promotes fusion and innovation. When we trust one another, we are able to combine our talents and skills to face whatever uncertainties lie ahead.

The bonds you make with others become immeasurable by numbers and contribute tremendously to each of our long-term positivity plans.

Finding happiness is much like setting out on a quest with your closest group of friends for a pot of gold at the end of the rainbow and knowing that there may be no pot of gold. What makes life beautiful, magical, and memorable are the people we share it with.

Listen Carefully

Everyone wants to be heard, but ironically not all of us are willing to be that person who listens.

The entire world is made up of signs and symbols that we explore in order to gain a sense of things and express ourselves. It might as well be described as an intricate web of meaning because causes and effects, reasoning and ideas, and movement are all too much information to take in at once. We invented language in order to get our points across much more efficiently, and although it helps with understanding messages on the surface, we have to consider that people have depth.

Our ears aren't detachable for a reason.

We may have been born with hearing, but we need to develop the skill of listening. It is usually coupled with observational skills, which entails more than just nodding at appropriate times and picking up keywords here and there. Understanding people's true intentions would call for you to put an emphasis on things like language, tone of voice, and pay attention to small slips that might give you an idea of what the person is really trying to indicate. This is not saying that you should unnecessarily mind people's business, but pay attention to them when you are directly concerned.

Genuine communication makes us feel good because it gives us a chance to relate ourselves to others. We yearn for that sense of belonging which may only be found in other people. Do not be afraid of people who can see your faults and do not judge them by theirs. Real listening paves the way for acceptance, which is the key ingredient to making the best things happen.

How do you cope with people who do not listen to you in return?

Grasping the meaning of "leave me alone" may vary in different situations. Although it might sound rude in print, speech has the ability to introduce other aspects of intention. Heeding the speaker's tone might draw you to make sounder conclusions on whether they may be in a hurry, scared, or tired. Considering the mood the speaker is in, as well as how you receive their message might give you a better chance of understanding the situation, and may be the best way to prevent conflict from happening.

Disputes take place because of misunderstandings, and have the potential to turn into larger issues that involve a lot more people. Take the concept of government as an example of different people having contrasting beliefs to achieve order. It would be difficult and unfair to the whole population if only one class benefited from the law. Although we are all entitled to our own stance, we still need to pay attention to other details in a situation to make the best decisions. Destructive habits like feeling overly competent or being easily offended by oppositions hinder us from growing and making connections with others. Do not underestimate each person's ability to understand the attitudes of others.

This might call for you to be more patient and open-minded about seeing where the other person is coming from. Maybe they might be under some kind of stress that makes them unable to hear you in return. We do not know what other things might be going on in their lives and are not in a position to find out. Try being still and steer clear of your opinions when you listen to others because some people may sense judgment in you and might feel that they are a waste of time.

You can be a great listener. All it takes is for you to put yourself in the place of the speaker and ask yourself how you would like them to receive your message if you were talking instead.

Approaching people in different ways can also be a good strategy to meet them even halfway. Sometimes, we have to put some distance to our perspective to see that a hill may not be a mountain. Good leaders don't lead by blindly giving out instructions but instead are concerned for the people in their care. Keeping silent and giving other people your time does not mean that you are passive, nor does it suggest that you are incapable of solving problems. It shows that you are humble and mature enough to admit that you can learn from others.

Being the last one in the room to speak has its perks.

Don't Compare Yourself With Others

A penny for your thoughts is completely out of the question if you have to pay loads more to get your sanity back.

People have created a world that constantly challenges us to question our own self-worth based on comparing ourselves with others. That has potentially developed into our most destructive habit.

Humans think in hierarchical patterns, and that reflects how our societies are built. The relationships between parents and kids, teachers and students, masters and pets all have the same notion that one being is superior to the other. Sometimes, deciphering these things allows us to piece facts about life into place. But if that endeavor affects and drains you emotionally and physically, then it may be time to reconsider your position in all this.

There may be some sense in relating ourselves to the world so that we may know who we are, but there are limits to that as well. Vanity and jealousy can be exhausting, yet they always seem to come as a packaged deal. Imagine trashing the best essay writer's paper in class so you could have a shot at getting the highest mark—sounds ugly, right? If you are jealous about what someone else has, chances are that this may be a reflection of your own insecurities.

Comparison is a sure ticket to discouragement and makes us exaggerate everything in the areas that we feel lacking in. You may easily turn your weight into a gigantic issue and dare to take unhealthy measures to settle yourself. Destructive habits always lead to more, and chances are that you might not ever think your body may be good enough if this habit continues.

A toxic workspace can be one of the most valid examples where comparison might work as the reigning principle, and sadly, this leads us to measure status superficially. Staying in those spaces may cause us to lose our passion for work and only be concerned about profit. This is why some of us make decisions so our boss won't yell at us. This is why we get distracted by other people's success.

Judging status by how successful a person may be in their career, how much money they make, and how perfect their love lives may be. This has nothing to do with the person they are on the inside. People show others what they want them to see as a defense mechanism to protect themselves from appearing as not good enough.

Media can be destructive to how we perceive ourselves and indirectly emphasize what we lack. Feeding ourselves more of it, without understanding what it can do to us, only increases the habit of affiliating ourselves with what we do not have. Do you know at least one person who is addicted to spending? Sometimes, it does not matter what they purchase, but they always seem to cave in when they get the itch. They might momentarily feel good about themselves and feel their status rise, but that does not usually last.

Reacting might not always be the best way to silence competition, but instead, sticking to your long-term vision gives you a better chance of focusing on what you need to do. The challenge is to be emotionally professional—learn from others and allow others to learn from you. Being professional does not mean wiping ourselves free from emotions, but being able to manage temperance to see what has to be done and cooperate with others if we need to.

Do not aim to be the best person in the room, but rather strive to be the best person that you can be.

Admiring somebody for a good quality that they have is a great way to deal with insecurities. Not only does it entail acceptance, which sets you free into the present moment, but it also fosters healthy competition. It gives you the peace of mind to focus on your own strengths and simultaneously get better at what others may be good at as well.

Grow your own strengths rather than be intimidated by others.

There is not going to be a better you than you.

See The Other Side Of Things

Flip a table upside down, and what you'll get is a plank attached to four wooden legs sticking up. We can drape a blanket over it and call it a fort, or we can wind some rope around it and call it a tiny wrestling ring.

A child's mind is incredibly malleable and absorbent, which means that learning and imagining things can be as easy as counting "one, two, three." They see the world through possibilities and are not much concerned about whether or not things are right or wrong. Because of this, they are more open to learning than we adults are and are more easily convinced about accepting differences.

Each person is entitled to their own unique perspective, and adding all that up amounts to the diversity we share amongst each other. It means more than just the color of our skins or the places that we grew up in. It pertains to each of our personalities and perspectives. Institutions like high school, work, and family life shapes us to be a solid representation of somebody. These things teach us to have our own opinions and be up to date with certain facts. As grownups, we may not experience the fluidity of thinking as much and tend to make decisions based on instinct or stocked knowledge. Although we are encouraged to strengthen our own individuality, we have to learn that this can be as limiting as it can be grounding.

If you have been to a university or college, you might notice that the experience amounts to more than the classroom lessons. It is a time to train yourself to stand on your own and with others. Living in a dorm teaches you independence and how to budget your money, and since not all classes might be held in a formal setting, your instructors and professors would also encourage you to develop your own views and solutions to certain subjects. In this learning space, you may realize that not everything is objective, that answers may vary, and that sometimes there may be no right answer.

Two people can equally be correct at something.

When you feel that you may be leaning to more than one option and are unsure what path to take, take a step back and try to see things for what they are. Then you can ask yourself why you perceive a situation as such and take it further by asking your questions in different ways.

For example, some of us may have trouble sleeping at night, and there are many available reasons for it—a busy mind, demanding jobs, or it may be a loud neighbor next door. Simply rephrasing "why you cannot sleep" to "what can make you sleep" changes the demands, and instantly gives you insights into different solutions. You may decide to contact your neighbor and kindly ask them to quiet down after a certain time, find other ways to manage your time, or get a better pillow. The options don't just end there, and you can think of more creative ways to get around certain complications.

Developing your own thinking strategies will allow you to take your life in new directions because certain tactics can match your abilities better. Following a standard only works until some point and should only serve as the basis for other matters to develop on. Eventually, you would have to learn how to adapt to changing times. You might discover yourself to be a generalist or realize that you love paying attention to details and use that to anchor your initial opinions before taking a second look around the situation to see if there are other factors to take in.

Learning how to disagree can be as valuable as seeing the other side of things, especially when pressing matters are at hand. Sometimes, we need answers that are on point and create boundaries to narrow down our options. Engaging in conversations with others may be the best way to expand your views, but it is also a good opportunity to know what does not apply. Allow yourself to think infinitely and see the patterns that are present in it.

You may realize that there is always more to something or somebody if you look closely, and people surprise us because they don't put everything on show. What we see might not be the whole truth, yet it draws us to confirm certain things.

An unpopular but often thought of belief is that wealthier people are happier and live a fuller life than people who are not—which is obviously not true. Material wealth is only one side to the story and is merely a surface detail. A rich family might have more comfort, but that does not entirely tell us what their relationship is with one another. There are lots of people who know what it is to work hard and pay attention to detail, who know how to listen to their friends, who care for their parents, and who can sincerely appreciate the small things in life, and they may not necessarily be millionaires. This is not saying that rich people are bad but it is an example of seeing the gray scales in the midst of black and white.

The truth is that some employers hire people not because they know what the job is about or have any experience in it, but because they are able to bring a new perspective to certain things. Creative teams do not only exist in the Arts, but can be applied in a business perspective as well. There are no fixed rules to strategy, and different solutions can be applicable at different times.

Nothing is absolute, and we can make innovation happen by being open to each other's differences and by showing respect.

Accept Change

There is no such thing as normal.

There may be times when we feel that we are in a good and safe position in life and that we do not want to let any of those circumstances go. Having a job that pays well, even though your heart may not be in it, could still be really difficult to move away from. Still, it may be best to keep in mind that someday things might not be the same. Only you can answer the question of what truly makes you happy in the long run.

Try to recall your purpose and vision.

This might not be applicable to everyone, but whether you may be thinking about taking your career in a different direction or deciding to take a relationship one step further, it might be best to compose yourself before asking why you are hesitant about making changes. When you have come to a considerable conclusion, you could then ask yourself how that change could benefit you and those around you and what may be the possible sacrifices you have to make. Being open to good and bad changes alike can cause alterations to your routines, and may call you to weigh the consequences to things that might not even happen. We all know that uncertainty can be exciting and daunting, but that does not necessarily mean that we should be reckless with our actions. When you feel that you have already made a suitable choice, try talking to others who you can trust to help you make bigger decisions.

Going with the flow of life does not entail passivity but the instinct to know the right time to act. Life shifts, transforms, and creates new experiences every day, but there are some things in life that we cannot control. Doing too much, or not being able to do enough, tears us apart, and instead of solving a problem, we end up losing our hold over a situation. Step back and take a breath, then ask yourself what and why you are doing this, which will hopefully help you prioritize your actions and thoughts.

So what happens if you accept change and others around you do not?

The truth is that you have to be alright with it for now because it may not be their time to move on just yet. You cannot promise them a reward for their efforts, nor can you force them into it. Just like yourself, the choice has to come from them. Still, it may be good practice to keep the curiosity going, help others understand that permanence cannot allow positive change to happen. After all, the memories that flash before our eyes at the end of our journey are the ones with the greatest emotional impact, and those happen because we believe in something greater than ourselves.

Change has the potential to bring out that creativity in you. A change in circumstances challenges others to do better while fostering innovation can generate surprisingly genius outputs. We are all aiming for that world where inclusion and diversity will allow each one of us to express ourselves freely. Getting there means that we all have to adapt to the changing times.

Things will not go back to the way they were, and we have to accept that.

Be Grateful About The Simple Things

Aiming high is not the problem, but rather what you are aiming for might be the more interesting question.

Mountains are magnificent sights to behold, but sometimes we tend to overlook certain details, like the soil and all the small rocks that give it form.

You may have already spent some time thinking about where you want to take your life. That always includes finding ways to make it better—and that's great news! Most of you might have been working on building healthier self-esteem to give you the courage and assurance of handling difficult tasks. You may also have brought yourself to widen your social circle and engage in more meaningful conversations. It will be delightful to know that you are setting higher standards for yourself, but as productive as you may be, you might also want to consider how you are shaping yourself.

When do you feel at your best? Does your answer include being promoted at work or gaining somebody's trust? Some of you might take pride in being responsible parents, while others may feel amazing when they put on some new shoes that they saved up for.

A reward does wait for us after most endeavors, like graduating college or being able to do flips on a skateboard after months of practice. It does help to be extra specific with what you want. It resembles the triumph we have over obstacles and an improvement in our skills. We all work hard, we all advance, and we feel good about ourselves when we achieve something, but the thing about life is that even the momentous things pass by, and once we accomplish a goal, we might as well be on our way to reach for a new one.

Trying to boost your self-esteem can become an addiction if it entails pressuring yourself to rise up to a superficial status. Money, popularity, and a skyrocketing career can be splendidly attractive and tempting to flaunt around. There is also no doubt that they might bring comfort to our living conditions, yet no matter how much we have of it, we may still be prone to hearing whispers at the back of our minds about wanting more. These things do not enforce any real relationships with other people, nor do they contribute to our development as a person. Giving a child a dollar to be good all day does not necessarily guarantee that they will behave, and chances are that promising a grownup a triple bonus at the end of the year if they make amazing sales has nothing to do with how they play the business game. Ambition ceases to become a fruitful endeavor when it destroys the relationship you have with yourself and with others.

Have you ever just stopped at a sidewalk to smell the flowers?

Gratefulness means turning back to the simple things in life and being thankful for them. Fresh air, clean water, delicious and nutritious food, and sunshine are all the basic necessities for each person to survive, while warm friendships and familial love all help bring out the best in us. Although they are outside factors, they are naturally part of life that we can benefit from forming bonds with.

Gratitude refocuses your attention towards what you already have so that you can make the best out of it. Improving your talents is like having your own garden—tending to every bud and leaf with enough water, sunshine, and love so that each plant grows and blossoms the way they were meant to. You cannot turn a rose into a peony, nor would it be ethical to nab a bush from your neighbor's lawn at night.

Do not be afraid of losing your talents or your virtues because nobody can ever take them from you. Creativity, innovation, pride, and discipline are likely to be unavailable at your local department store, which means that you would just have to whip it up yourself.

Learn to appreciate the journey that you are going through, and it will lead you to see abundance in life.

Connect With Nature

No matter how deeply urban or contemporary some of us may consider ourselves to be, we all come from the very same place—life.

Nature surrounds us and is the very fabric of who we are. We are made of energy, from the very last cell in our bodies to the slightest thoughts in our minds. As much as it is a gift to be alive and experience the world, we sometimes need to actively reach out to it all.

We live in an age of fast-paced technology, where minutes and seconds seem less of what they are. For some of us who are living in the city, we might feel that life passes too quickly, are tired and overworked, and are missing our full potential. Taking a break from your surroundings, which includes being in your homes. Going outdoors can make wondrous changes to your lifestyle. It gives you time to unwind and ground yourself back to where you came from.

For us to fully engage with our natural surroundings, it may be best to learn how to disconnect from other aspects of our lives. Being at two places at one time does not only happen physically but can pertain to our thoughts drifting away when we are somewhere else. This might call for you to be a little stricter with yourself and make physical restrictions like putting your phone away during meals, the hours nearing bedtime, when you are in a conversation, or when you are just outside in general. Try until they become good habits because all of this is to help you gain a stronger sense of connection.

We need others to survive, but we need our world just as much.

Reconnecting with nature unlocks our single-point perspective. Not only may we be pleased with the look of our surroundings, but we have the potential to discover many new things. A stroll around your neighborhood can be the most convenient place to get up and move around. Trees, grass, the sky, the small animals—each have their own character and move in different ways. It might be nice to get along with some of our neighbors and talk about something other than the weather. Forming social bonds improves our emotional status and can prevent us from experiencing depression. Grab this opportunity to fill your life with people, and get inspiration for just about anything!

The outdoors can be a wonderful place to spend your pastime. Apart from getting fresh air, hobbies like gardening could be something you could look forward to after a busy day in front of a monitor. Whether you plant flowers, herbs, or grow a tree, seeing them grow still makes us feel satisfied. Plants are quite sure of themselves as they grow at their own pace and blossom into what they were meant to be. There is a peace in them that we all can learn from.

Understanding life's story also entails receiving its blessings. Sunshine is our planet's source of energy and is famously known to supply us with vitamin D. We need this to keep our muscles and bones strong. The older we get, the slower it might be for our bodies to absorb and process vitamin D from sunshine. This may lead to getting bone fractures and acquiring osteoporosis. It may be best to get hiking from where you are at; that will help transition you better into old age. The best time to get it is early in the morning, so for all those late risers out there, seeing the world in a different light might be something you could add to your bucket list!

You may also want to consider plotting your schedule to squeeze in some definite time being outdoors. It may ease you to know that your time is carefully allotted and that you would not be missing other things in your schedule.

Being with nature holds us to our senses and helps us think about things more clearly. It may be sort of like getting a life check, with the guarantee of experiencing emotional healing.

We need to put ourselves out in the world in order to know our place in it. In time, we may all be able to let go and see things for what they really are.

Surround Yourself With Loved Ones

Life is best spent with the people you love.

Sharing a joke, having a meal, and crying about a bad day—they all feel better when they are shared with someone special.

We were just not made to survive by ourselves in this wide world, and we all know that we need the love and support of others to make the best out of our lives. We have the natural tendency to give just as we take, and what better way to keep that cycle going with the most eclectic and good-humored troop we can muster?

We all know the value of true friends and family because these people show us their own side to things. A mother, a childhood friend, and even an instructor all exhibit their concern for us in various ways and are people with whom we can share different aspects of our lives. It does not suggest that one is better than the other, but the fact that we spend time in other places means that we are surrounded by different people. Some people just understand certain experiences more than others because we might have gone through it with them.

Studies in positive psychology have shown that the key ingredient to living a happy life and being more productive is to build a healthier social life. Feeling the support of others makes us feel safe and helps us develop healthy self-esteem. Apart from an exchange of knowledge, taking on rough challenges might not appear too scary because we know that other people have our backs. Good leaders could not run a nation without loyal supporters, just as star players in a team do not rise to victory without the help of their other members. Life is a collaborative endeavor and constantly in motion to make sure each of us has a moment to share our story.

Each of our lives affect one another, so sometimes we have to step back a bit to let other people take the spotlight.

Empathy is the deepest form of understanding that entails hearing what a person has to say as well as sympathizing with their experiences. It takes a great deal of self-sacrifice to make another person feel important, just as it might feel just as bad to see someone you care about go through a rough situation where all you can do is listen. Helping somebody out does not mean that you should solve their problems for them, but rather have confidence in them so they can have confidence in themselves. Sometimes, staying silent and being there for them can be the best gift you can give.

With so many distractions around us, we might not have all the resources to sit down and truly get to know everyone who comes along. It may also be possible that some of us might have fallen into the trap of toxic relationships and are unsure about whether or not we can take the pressures from them. If you feel that you may not be in the right headspace to deal with them, you can take some time off to collect yourself and then come back to answer some questions that might help you gauge if these people are true.

You will know from how they treat you, and feel that they want only the best things for you—even if they themselves might be struggling.

They are kind.

They respect you—your time, your efforts, your abilities, your feelings, and opinions.

They make you feel loved, regardless of your shortcomings.

They want you to be happy.

They are the ones who would still make time for you if you reached out to them at ungodly hours. They enjoy your company regardless of what your status is and are there for you when you feel that you are at your lowest point.

There is no such thing as the "right people" or the "wrong people" to spend our lives with. We can fall in love with their imperfections because it sets them apart from other people. You do not stop befriending someone just because he is not tech-savvy, or make up your mind one day to cut connections with your cousin because she keeps tripping over. In time, those little quirks can turn endearing and become what you remember them by. Chances are that those people love you for the same reasons—whatever that may be.

These people are treasures, and they are going to be your happiness.

Forgive

Forgiveness is like getting a refund for something you didn't sign up for—you let go of the bad stuff.

We all carry a certain amount of emotional pain that potentially affects our outlook on life. Feeling hurt or disappointed at something that did not turn out the way it was planned does manifest for others to see it in us, nor is it a pleasing sensation. Grudges, bitterness, and spite all lead to anger and suffering, which may be directed to others or to ourselves. Have you ever been in an argument with someone who equally refused to back down? How did that turn out?

Aggression ties people together just as closely as affection does but on a different level. There are cases when people refuse to let go of certain matters until they prove that they are right—and sadly disputes like these usually last longer than they intend to. Have you ever been in a family feud? Some might stretch on for generations because one party thinks they are better than the other. Each side might intensify the matter by involving other family members. Without respectfully coming to terms with the people who are directly affected by the issue, the root of the problem would still remain unsolved. The funny thing is that people might not even remember why they fought in the first place.

Forgiveness is a choice.

We are imaginative by nature, and that means our minds are always going to find excuses to justify ourselves. Feeling the need to fight back and reclaim your sense of status for any misunderstandings might be your initial defensive reaction. But thinking about the consequences after you make your move could save you from moments of affliction. Not only would you have destroyed your relationship with the person you are facing, but you also risk separating yourself from their circle of friends as well.

In times when you feel the dire need to justify yourself, try to think of all the better things you could be doing instead of sitting in on a fight.

Forgiveness can tremendously lift your feelings of burden and help you see reason. It entails letting go of mistakes, hurts, and some misconceptions you made along the way. You may not be at fault, but rudely calling others out for their mistakes makes you partially share the blame. It may be unlikely for people to do something if they are not willing to, and you might just be the same. Think about how you would like to be treated if you messed up and ask yourself what could convince you to feel at ease in that kind of situation.

Forgiving and forgetting may not always come hand in hand, while the latter might be considered the toughest part of moving past negative situations. Once we live through an experience, it somehow just sticks with us. The challenge here is to see the bigger picture, and that sometimes means putting yourself in other people's shoes. This would call you to take responsibility for your actions, which means that you may take credit for all the amazing things that you did, but you also have to deal with the consequences of your mistakes.

Life is full of unexpected moments, and there might be times when the knowledge we acquire along the way might be of no help to us. Awareness allows you to engage with the present moment and will enable you to work around it as you go. Although we may have all been advised to ditch the habit of cramming before an exam, we might have to rely on our human skills to pass through life. If you cannot help yourself to let go of hurtful experiences at the moment, it might be best to take some time to collect yourself. Distancing yourself to a certain limit usually helps you cool off from that memory, as well as keeping busy and improving yourself in any way that you can. When you are ready, you can try forgiving the smaller things first before you make your way towards larger matters.

Set yourself free, and use that time to create the life you want.

Write About Your Experiences

Our life experiences are like precious treasures that we keep locked up in our memory bank, but sometimes it may be impossible to fish them out. There are just too many good things to remember, and the most primal thing we can do is to jot them down!

We all experience human moments when we realize that the world is so much bigger than we are and that we need to take some more time to learn about it. A memory, whether good or bad, encapsulates our senses and allows us to re-experience that event on a mental level. Although our minds do have the ability to keep all that information, it might be difficult for us to bring all of them to the surface. Our minds forget in order to deal with trauma from strong negative emotions and when we just don't experience an emotional connection to certain events. Nonetheless, your ability to focus on the positive is what really matters, and writing about it is what can get you to see yourself from a distance.

Writing about your experiences can be a wonderful way to remember those great memories. While pictures and videos can serve as a more tangible way of retracing your steps, looking back at the good times through your personal perspective may be more intimate. It can also turn into a creative endeavor!

Writing, journaling, and scrapbooking can be ways to express yourself. It gives you access to delve deeper into your view of things and improve your memory. It can be a healthy space where you can think about the expectations you have for yourself and for others, as well as note down new interests and goals that you would set out for. Apart from that, writing also teaches you to be a better communicator and develop vocabulary and grammar.

Have you ever noticed that reading the same book at different stages in your life gives you the ability to see and understand things that you missed out on before?

We have all been through blissful and rough experiences alike.

In cases where you still carry heavy emotional baggage about someone or something, venting through writing can be a great way to just let it all out—and the good news is that no one has to hear about it! Writing a letter to someone with whom you might not be on good terms at the moment allows you to release your feelings without pulling on strings. It gives you the opportunity to explain yourself and retrace your thoughts right after. Sometimes, re-reading your letter might help you fill in some gaps in your feelings and help you recall details of a situation that happened before.

Take this chance to communicate with yourself, apart from just thinking about things.

Be A Blessing To Others

There is no such thing as a love shortage.

Compassion and generosity are not things bound by matter, nor are they measured by scales and numbers. When we truly love and care for someone, there just seems to be no bounds to how much time we would like to spend with them. Best friends don't get bored with each other for the reason that they are always there for each other.

Have you ever experienced the need for a big, warm hug to make you feel better when things get a little rough?

It is in our human nature to be with one another, and our main senses give us that chance to form emotions and ideas by experiencing what is around us. Our sense of touch not only allows us to interact with our environment and is our body's first line of defense, but it also lets us feel compassion. We are biologically designed to relate to and make an impact on one another. You are definitely not the only person in this world who is searching for long and lasting happiness. Look around, and you may find that others might just be on the same journey.

Life is about making connections and sharing your talents and positivity with the world. Human skills pertain to the qualities we need to make connections with others, like being able to love, trust, and rely on somebody. We feel completeness in others by experiencing a surge of oxytocin when we come in physical contact with people, like hugs and pats on the back, and are able to form genuine relationships with one another. Women who give birth undergo a huge gush of oxytocin, and that is what is responsible for the special bond they have with their children. We also can get oxytocin through acts of kindness, like sharing a meal or just being there for someone who feels down.

Things just keep getting better from there.

Having more oxytocin in your system boosts your immunity, increases your problem-solving abilities, creativity, and prevents addiction. Since our bodies continuously try to repeat habits that make us feel good, we begin to develop the tendency of being more generous. We all have the opportunity to live a happy and long life, and it comes with being there for others.

Seeing the true value in another person is being genuine about your intentions to help and not looking to gain favor afterward. Be there to give and not to get the crowd's applause later. We live in a society where distance happens at an emotional level more than it does physically, which is ironic of the situation that we are in. Technology has distracted most of us from having meaningful conversations with one another. Being famous ceases to have value without giving any contribution to your community, while craving for emotional assurance on a digital platform can be just as fleeting as switching tabs.

Remove those filters, and see the world for its true colors.

Patience, kindness, being able to listen, and empathy are skills you need to know in order to handle difficult and sensitive conversations. We may all be faced with the dilemma of being with someone in their darkest hours, and honestly, it might be even more painful seeing them in trouble than dealing with it ourselves. Not having the solution to their problems is a sick feeling, and it might make us feel guilty to just sit and listen.

The answer to this is that you should let them figure things out for themselves.

Help others stand on their own and develop themselves according to their own strengths. This does not mean letting them take advantage of you by doing all the dirty work because that would burn you out and base the relationship on insincerity. Do not try to fix their problems because you do not have the in-depth experience of their situation as they do. Be there for them by listening, and they will have a sense that they are not alone.

The more you spend time with people, the more you may see that your actions and words ripple off into feelings, behavior, and finally impact on the other person's life. Be a blessing to others so that they may find the strength to feel complete and sure of themselves.

You do not break people to get the most out of them—that just leaves them with trauma and contempt for you. Tough love is not a fact and in no way helps a person achieve personal growth. It is also a false way to gain respect and creates more space for social distance—and we really don't need that. If someone is being unreasonable to you, try to first see things from their point of view. Talking and being honest about your feelings usually does help others connect with you. It might take some time for things to settle in nicely, but no matter what reaction you get, always remember to be respectful.

Approaching these last steps to live a happier life requires you to build genuine relationships with others. If you cannot bring yourself to share happiness with others, chances are that you may return to destructive old habits. You do not lose anything when you are able to help someone be the best version of themselves, but rather you are working your way to becoming the best version of yourself as well.

Be that person who sees the spark in others that no one else can.

Be that person who teaches others to live a life of gratitude and keep the cycle of graces going around.

Be that person who supports others and gives them the encouragement to finish their mission.

Keep Moving On

Regardless of what stage of life you are in, we are all on the same path that keeps us moving forward.

Life is going to take us places and continue on after us—but that isn't anything to shed a tear for. Be happy, remember? This is what we all went through to accept.

Your pursuit of happiness has been splendid, and surely you have made remarkable habits that push yourself up and allow you to express yourself for who you are. We have all learned the value of self-love and the power of counting on one another. We know that our bodies were made to experience happiness and that peace and joy can be found within us. It would not hurt to retrace these steps once in a while, just in case we need a little reminder before we can be on our way again to build a better world.

Keep your mind on the possibilities that lie ahead!

We all can choose to live the best life that we can and share it with others. Learning from our past and savoring each present moment is all we can do for now. Taking that first, big step into the unknown might as well be the next life-changing move you can make from the things you have gone through before.

We all make mistakes, we laugh, we give, and we love, and do it all over again.

We can keep on trying, and looking towards each other for support.

We all have a chance at living a good life, and it all depends on how much you want it to happen.

So, how is that life plan you have been working on?

Conclusion

Happiness is abundant by nature and can be found within ourselves.

Some people may identify it as a mood or an emotion, while others who are more experienced with the essence of life may characterize it as a way of living. It is first and foremost an abstract sensation that we associate with certain positive experiences, like attaining personal achievements and by sharing love and companionship with others. Happiness has a full effect on our overall well-being, such as our physical and mental health as well as our productivity levels, and can potentially affect how we interact with the world around us. Ultimately, it is a state of mind that entails being at peace with yourself in the present moment.

Happiness that lasts is something that we all wish for, but sometimes the situations around us have the ability to greatly shift and manipulate our feelings. How we conduct ourselves in times of crisis may determine how our bodies cope with stress. Knowing what it means to be truly happy, as well as prioritizing certain things that make each one of us better people, can increase our chances of living a happy life and help us form better connections with others. Being able to decipher genuine opportunities that make us grow as individuals apart from fleeting thrills that can only provide excitement for a certain period of time would require strength and self-control to refrain from submitting ourselves to these impulses.

We are all capable of experiencing a sense of positivity even in life's darkest hours, and it all depends on how we choose to look at a situation.

Harboring positive and focused thoughts can be extremely effective when it comes to self-motivation. Be patient and kind with yourself, and understand that it takes time to heal yourself from discouraging experiences. Rid yourself from self-destructive habits, like comparing your abilities with others and criticizing yourself for not being good enough. Grab the opportunity to help yourself become the best person that you can be because that is the best way to live life.

Working with a purpose gives us all something to look forward to, and it can be exciting if we get to share that experience with others. Your purpose can belong to others just as much. Since we are visually driven beings by nature, it may be best to write down your ideas or plot a to-do list to strengthen the effectiveness of your intentions. Developing a positive mindset that allows you to focus on your good goals can be a way to clear your mind from outside pressures. Try not to stress yourself out about chasing happiness because 0f the ideal life that you are searching for lies just in front of you. By being aware of the present moment, you may find it easier to develop your talents and skills and end up being more flexible in handling tricky situations. By trusting yourself and loving yourself, you are beginning to open yourself up to your full potential.

Transitioning from happy thoughts to happy actions can be a great way to experience and explore the bigger world out there. Taking care of your physical body is just as important as caring for your mind, and it brings balance to your life. Doing small things like getting enough rest, moving around, and eating nutritious foods not only keeps your physical body in shape but protects your immune system as well. Engaging in a hobby that you enjoy can be one of the most effective ways to destress from a busy schedule. It also gives you the opportunity to unleash your creativity and discover new things about yourself.

Set aside some time each day to be with yourself. Ideally, it would be nice if you could distance yourself from outside noise to collect your thoughts and reflect on your feelings. At the same time, try not to let any negative ideas cloud your mind or take over your emotional state. Do yourself the favor of expressing yourself through your talents and strengths, as it is the best way to exercise your individuality.

The paradox of living a life of happiness entails for you to find it within yourself and seeing how your actions connect and contribute to changes happening around you. Existence is infinite, and it takes a certain awakening in our consciousness to realize how beautiful and good life can actually be. Despite hardships and trials, we still have the power to get past each one of them by trusting in ourselves and getting help from others. We all want to improve and grow as individuals, as well as feel that we belong with the people in our community. Reaching out to others once we have learned to make peace with ourselves can be the best way to sustain that happiness. Be grateful for who you are, both your strengths and weaknesses, as well as enjoy the company of those who love you.

Let go of the memories that make you feel less than who you are, do what you can today to be the best person that you can be, and keep moving on.

Gratitude

Gratitude is a powerful feeling that allows us to be at peace with ourselves and our place in reality. Not only is it a virtue that we associate with being thankful for whatever we have at the moment, but it can also be transformed into a mindset that helps us refocus our attention towards the things that really matter. It is taking a step back from the little space we occupy to realize that there is so much more in this world that can be experienced and explored.

The world today can be full of social pressures that somehow convince us to feel unsatisfied with ourselves. We tend to look outwards for satisfaction instead of nurturing our mind and body, and end up measuring our self-worth with everything that we do not have. The influential power of media, which is most relevant to our society today, functions on the principles of consumerism that seduces us with the need to acquire more of certain things to be complete. Wanting to increase our status can turn into a sickness that stretches out into a long, unending spree of comparing yourself to others while acquiring so many material things leaves you feeling empty inside because you have not actually grown emotionally or socially in any way. Slowly going back to the basics of appreciating the simple things in life, like fresh air, clean water, and sunshine, not only rids you from a superficially charged mentality but allows you to fully engage with the real world.

We are all made as a whole and complete, and each of us is gifted with our own set of personalities and abilities. Our personal characteristics are worth more than anything that can be purchased in a shop, so take each day as an opportunity to grow and reach out further to life's experiences. Being truly grateful for your talents and skills and the people who love and care for you can surprisingly bring you at ease against the pressures of society and can help you focus on the positive side of things.

The more you count your blessings, the more you may realize that your list of things to be grateful for can turn out to be limitless as well. Life is an unending cycle of give and take, so save yourself from worrying about not having enough and be a blessing to others.

Sharing

Happiness and positivity are meant to be shared, especially with the people you love.

As social beings, we all have the need to form connections with one another. Family, being the basic unit of society, is a structure that reflects our social patterns of support, communication, and personal identification. There is no use denying that we all share that sense of belonging and comradery. People are important because they have the ability to inspire and motivate us to be a better version of ourselves, as well as comfort us in times of discouragement and uncertainty. We are all a part of life and are responsible for the connections that bind and affect the opportunities for the people around us. We are all capable of creating harmonious relationships with one another, and building a brighter future for the generations to come. It takes a certain amount of humility to accept that our individual selves are not the only things that matter in this life and that keeping to the flow of graces can actually amplify our individual purpose.

Sharing is not limited to material goods, like money or presents, but can be emulated in acts of kindness and generosity. Giving our time and attention to others can be the greatest gift of all because it allows us to grow emotionally and socially by forming genuine relationships with others. We generally feel a sense of accomplishment when we are able to help others realize their potential and worth. Helping somebody out can make us feel incredibly joyful, while our actions can encourage other people to embody that same attitude towards others.

Putting a little bit of happiness in everything that we do can surprisingly go a long way and make major changes to the way we see things. We can all lend a helping hand to one another so that others may also have the opportunity to see and experience life in full color.

Life seems momentary when we look back and see how far we have come, so make the best of what we can today and turn them into memories that stand out tomorrow!

References

Ciotti, G. (n.d.). *The Psychological Benefits of Writing*. Help Scout: https://www.helpscout.com/blog/benefits-of-writing/

Davis, T. (2021). *How Your Imagination Can Help You Feel More Positive*. Shine: https://advice.theshineapp.com/articles/how-your-imagination-can-help-you-feel-more-positive/

Grant, A. (2013). *Give and Take*. New York: Penguin Group.

Jaekl, P. (2017). *Here's What Happens in Your Brain When Your Life Flashes Before Your Eyes*. The Cut: https://www.thecut.com/2017/01/what-it-means-when-your-life-flashes-before-your-eyes.html

Jeremiah, D. (2004). *31 Days to Happiness*. W Publishing Group.

Jeremiah, D. (2017). *A Life Beyond Amazing*. HarperCollins.

Just Move! The Six Benefits of Everyday Movement. (2020). Anschutz Health and Wellness Center:

https://anschutzwellness.com/just-move-benefits-everyday-movement/

Leanse, E. P. (2017). *The Happiness Hack*. Naperville, Illinois: Simple Truths.

Lyubomirsky, S. (2013). *The Myths of Happiness*. New York: The Penguin Press.

Markowitz, M. (n.d.). *When Relatives Attack*. Reader's Digest: https://www.rd.com/jokes/family/

Mayo Clinic Staff. (2020). *Forgiveness: Letting Go of Grudges and Bitterness*. Mayo Clinic: https://www.mayoclinic.org/healthy-lifestyle/adult-health/in-depth/forgiveness/art-20047692

Murphey, D. (n.d.). *How to Reconnect with Nature for Better Mental Health*. Skills You Need : https://www.skillsyouneed.com/rhubarb/reconnect-nature.html

Raypole, C. (2020). *How to Forgive Someone (Even If They Really Screwed Up)*. Healthline: https://www.healthline.com/health/how-to-forgive#when-to-start

Raypole, C. (2021). *Can't Remember Your Childhood? What Might Be Going On*. Healthline: https://www.healthline.com/health/why-cant-i-remember-my-childhood#takeaway.

www.ingramcontent.com/pod-product-compliance
Lightning Source LLC
Chambersburg PA
CBHW060816050426
42449CB00008B/1688